BUILDING MY VOCABULARY

OPPOSITES

LET'S READ AV2 BY WEIGL™ ADDED VALUE • AUDIO VISUAL

by Dayna Martin

www.av2books.com

Go to **www.av2books.com,** and enter this book's unique code.

BOOK CODE

AVX76949

AV^2 by Weigl brings you media enhanced books that support active learning.

AV^2 provides enriched content that supplements and complements this book. Weigl's AV^2 books strive to create inspired learning and engage young minds in a total learning experience.

Your AV^2 Media Enhanced books come alive with...

Audio
Listen to sections of the book read aloud.

Video
Watch informative video clips.

Embedded Weblinks
Gain additional information for research.

Try This!
Complete activities and hands-on experiments.

Key Words
Study vocabulary, and complete a matching word activity.

Quizzes
Test your knowledge.

Slide Show
View images and captions, and prepare a presentation.

... and much, much more!

Published by AV^2 by Weigl
350 5th Avenue, 59th Floor New York, NY 10118
Website: www.av2books.com

Library of Congress Cataloging-in-Publication Data

Names: Martin, Dayna, 1983- author.
Title: Opposites / Dayna Martin.
Description: New York, NY : AV2 by Weigl, [2019] | Series: Building my vocabulary
Identifiers: LCCN 2018053465 (print) | LCCN 2018058015 (ebook) | ISBN 9781489696359 (Multi User Ebook) | ISBN 9781489696366 (Single User Ebook) | ISBN 9781489696335 (hc : alk. paper) | ISBN 9781489696342 (pbk. : alk. paper)
Subjects: LCSH: English language--Synonyms and antonyms--Juvenile literature. | Vocabulary--Juvenile literature.
Classification: LCC PE1591 (ebook) | LCC PE1591 .M363 2018 (print) | DDC 428.1--dc23
LC record available at https://lccn.loc.gov/2018053465

Printed in the United States of America in Brainerd, Minnesota
1 2 3 4 5 6 7 8 9 0 22 21 20 19 18

122018
102918

First published by Engage Books in 2015

Project Coordinator: Priyanka Das Designer: A.R. Roumanis

The publisher acknowledges Shutterstock as the primary image supplier for this title.

OPPOSITES

by Dayna Martin

Up

Down

In

Out

Big Small

Clean

Dirty

Empty

Full

Safe

Dangerous

Hot

Cold

Wet

Dry

Long

Short

Slow Fast

Few

Many

Front

Back

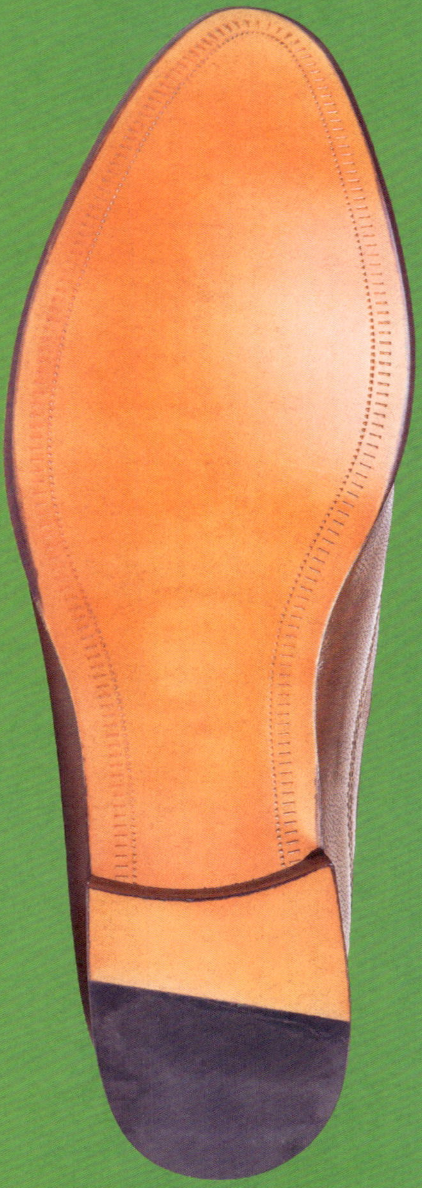

Smooth

Rough

Hard Soft

Heavy

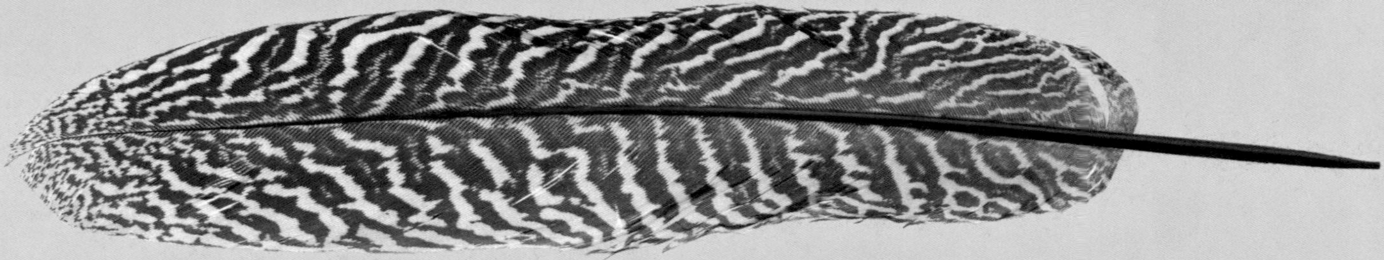

Light

Sit

Stand

Above

Below

Loose

Tight

Young

Old

New

Old

On

Off

Open

Closed

Tall Short

Near

Far

Asleep

Awake

Dark

Light

Thick

Thin

Happy

Sad

Opposites activity

Do you remember what these opposites are called? Can you find **heavy/light, in/out, hot/cold,** and **hard/soft**? Match the opposites.

Answer: in

Answer: soft

Answer: light

Answer: heavy

Answer: cold

Answer: out

Answer: hot

Answer: hard